THE BOOK OF ROSÉ

THE PROVENÇAL VINEYARD
THAT REVOLUTIONIZED ROSÉ

THE BOOK OF ROSÉ

THE PROVENÇAL VINEYARD
THAT REVOLUTIONIZED ROSÉ

by Whispering Angel and Château d'Esclans

TEXTS BY
LINDSEY TRAMUTA

PHOTOGRAPHY BY
MARTIN BRUNO

RIZZOLI
NEW YORK

New York · Paris · London · Milan

"The peoples of the Mediterranean began to emerge from barbarism when they learned to cultivate olive trees and vines."

Thucyclides, fifth century BCE

The world of wine has always been full of pioneers. From the very first person to crush grapes beneath their feet, ferment the juice and create a rosy ambrosia more than 2,500 years ago, there have been enterprising winemakers committed to channeling the gifts of the land and sharing them broadly.

The greatest icons in wine-industry history know that behind every innovation is a deep understanding of terroir and an uncompromising commitment to their beliefs. Much like shifting culture, pushing the boundaries of taste and viticulture requires courage, time to finesse breakthrough ideas, and a certain level of comfort with risk and resistance.

If anyone has harnessed these qualities to successfully disrupt convention in wine it is Sacha Lichine, the visionary owner of Château d'Esclans, the global reference in Provençal rosé. Twenty years ago, rosé was considered an unserious wine that lacked the prestige and respect of red and white AOP wines (AOP, or *Appellation d'origine contrôlée*, are standards that control the production of wine, spirits, and other agricultural products). It was thought to be saccharine and unpolished, an afterthought among producers and an elusive sell outside of the picturesque restaurants of Saint-Tropez. Today, it is nothing short of a cultural phenomenon, dominated by the dry, accessible, and refreshing style popularized by Sacha Lichine and his founding consulting oenologist, Patrick Léon.

As you will read in these pages, this is the tale of how one man and a team of experts heeded their instincts, nurtured the land, took considerable risks, and boldly launched a revolution to elevate rosé to a fine wine and a multimillion-dollar business. Like all the best rosés, the story begins in Provence.

Opposite: A book of memories and family legacy. Sacha Lichine's Château d'Esclans, the global reference in Provençal rosé.

SETTING THE SCENE: WINEMAKING IN PROVENCE

LONG BEFORE IT WAS SYNONYMOUS WITH SUMMER INSOUCIANCE, MORE THAN THREE HUNDRED DAYS OF SUNSHINE PER YEAR, SWATHS OF LAVENDER FIELDS, AND ROLLING VINEYARDS, THE REGION KNOWN TODAY AS PROVENCE WAS, FIRST AND FOREMOST, THE BIRTHPLACE OF FRENCH CIVILIZATION. SIGNS OF ANCIENT HUMAN LIFE THROUGHOUT THE SOUTH OF FRANCE, SUCH AS CAVE PAINTINGS AND ENGRAVINGS, STRETCH BACK HUNDREDS OF THOUSANDS OF YEARS.

Previous pages: The lush lavender fields of Provence.
Above and opposite: The beauty of Provence: the hilltop village of Gordes (above)
and the sun-drenched port town of Cassis (opposite).

Above: Amid the vines south of Château d'Esclans,
with parasol pine trees looming large. **Opposite:** The French Riviera, coastal neighbor
of Château d'Esclans. **Following pages:** Sacha Lichine knew, just by looking, that he would
one day own a rosé vineyard in this rich expanse of the Esclans Valley.

"WHAT CHAMPAGNE IS TO SPARKLING, IS WHAT PROVENCE IS TO ROSÉ."

Sacha Lichine

Opposite: The historic vines for rosé at Château d'Esclans.

At the end of the last glacial period, or a mere twenty thousand years ago, wild grape and olive vines took root on the edge of the Mediterranean and provided sustenance to the age's hunter-gatherers. What was collected by humans in one era was cultivated as an agricultural staple in another—particularly in Mesopotamia and along the Nile Delta, between the fifth and sixth millennium BCE.

Various groups—from the Ligurians and Celtics to the Phocaeans (Greeks from the city of Phocaea)—settled in the areas between Orange, Marseille (or ancient Massilia), and Menton on the modern-day Riviera before the Romans descended and conquered the land at the end of the second century BCE. By that time, the Phocaeans had established the earliest grapevines on the territory and were already creating rosé by crushing red and white grapes and fermenting the juice in clay vessels.

Opposite: Grapes growing on the vineyards of Château d'Esclans are used to produce the wines that are made for the Estate Collection, which includes Château d'Esclans, Les Clans, and Garrus, as well as a portion of the grapes used to produce Rock Angel. **Following pages:** A lush gradient of green on the flatter swath of vines located south of the Château.

The Romans took the process further by planting vineyards and turning the region, then known as Provincia, into the first veritable Roman province outside of Italy. Up to the late fifteenth century, the region was ruled by the Counts of Provence, until the title was passed to Louis XI of France, officially making it French.

The winemaking tradition became a pillar of the Provençal identity not only as a result of foreign influence but of the region's ideal conditions—the Mediterranean climate, with its warm, dry summer days and relatively cool evenings, mild winters, strong breezes, like the mistral, that sweep away pests and clear the air, as well as consistent sunshine—which created the perfect foundation for producing wine. Add to this the region's natural rocky hillside soil that is rich in clay and limestone, which allows the grapes to proliferate more easily, and all the essential viticultural elements are in place.

Still, it takes a special human touch to capture the essence and beauty of the eminently casual Provençal lifestyle and express it—one bottle at a time—through wine.

Opposite: The easygoing Provençal way of life at Château d'Esclans.
Following pages: The property's hundred-year-old plane trees in the summer sun.

WAKING
A SLEEPING BEAUTY

WITH SUCH A RICH HERITAGE, PROVENCE IS NATURALLY FERTILE
TERRAIN FOR PRODUCING EXCEPTIONAL WINES. BUT NOT ALL
THE WINES, NOR THE PRODUCTION STORIES BEHIND THEM,
ARE CREATED EQUAL. THE STORY OF THE CHÂTEAU D'ESCLANS
RENAISSANCE, AND WHAT SETS IT APART FROM THE REST, IS
ONE OF FAMILY LEGACY. IT'S A STORY OF UNMATCHED VISION
AND BOLD RISK-TAKING THAT REVOLUTIONIZED AND INFLUENCED
AN ENTIRE DRINKING CULTURE.

acha Lichine was born into French wine royalty. His father, the late Alexis Lichine, was the most esteemed authority of French wine in the United States for more than forty years. Nicknamed the "Pope of Wine," the Russian émigré, author, educator, and wine importer single-handedly introduced and evangelized French wine to a postwar, post-prohibition American market that had long been dominated by hard spirits, cocktails, and beers—everything but wine.

Alexis Lichine, who first discovered wine in Paris, landed in New York in 1934 to a nonexistent wine market bursting with opportunity. In true American fashion, Lichine assumed the role of the quintessential traveling salesman, traversing the country by Greyhound bus, going door-to-door spreading the gospel of the grape. He sought out the most influential decision-makers, from private collectors to restaurants and sommeliers, from clubs to hotels, including the Waldorf-Astoria. Thanks to Lichine's tenacious efforts, the iconic hotel began selling more French grand cru wines than any other property in the world.

Previous pages: After first visiting the Château in 1994, Sacha Lichine made it his own in 2006 to transform the world of rosé. **Opposite:** Moving day at the freshly renovated Château d'Esclans.

With the market in rapid growth by 1950, the Lichine name took on widespread resonance. Wine writer David Lincoln Ross once remarked that buying wine with the Lichine label was not only chic but a gauge of quality for an American consumer who still felt behind the curve when it came to matters of wine and gastronomy. The consumer looked not only to France but to those with great knowledge for guidance on savoir vivre—and still do to this day.

Having proven himself as the authority on the matter, Lichine took the next logical step to expand his influence by establishing a prestigious wine estate of his own. He would take over not one but two properties in Bordeaux in 1951 and 1952, less than a decade before Sacha was born: Château Lascombes (second classified growth) and Château Prieuré-Lichine (formerly Prieuré-Cantenac), a fourth classified growth. While Château Lascombes eventually changed hands during Sacha's childhood, the future wine mogul was imbued in the aura of Château Prieuré-Lichine. At the Prieuré, Alexis Lichine played host to the world's cultural and political cognoscenti, breaking bread with everyone from Orson Welles to David and Laurance Rockefeller to Grace Kelly. It was in similarly rarefied company and environs that Sacha experienced a series of firsts: his first Bacchanalian romp as a young boy; his first sips of rosé alongside his father at the Hôtel de Paris Monte-Carlo one summer; and, his first driving lesson on the Prieuré estate—on a tractor. "Everything formative that happened around wine, I learned from my father," he says emphatically. "I knew wine would be in my future one way or another."

From top to bottom, and left to right:
Alexis Lichine tastes and examines bottles
during the harvest at Château Prieuré-
Lichine. — On American radio being
interviewed about *The Joy of Wine*, his
narrative album. — Holding *Encyclopedia
of Wines and Spirits*, his book, amongst
the first authoritative of its kind. —
At the Tastevin Grower's Lunch, in
Burgundy. — With the Haskells, US Wine
Trade visitors, at Château Lascombes.

"EVERYTHING FORMATIVE THAT HAPPENED AROUND WINE, I LEARNED FROM MY FATHER. I KNEW WINE WOULD BE IN MY FUTURE ONE WAY OR ANOTHER."

Sacha Lichine

Opposite: Alexis Lichine, the "Pope of Wine," who single-handedly introduced and evangelized French wine to the postwar American public. Lichine always believed that "the best way to learn about wine is by tasting."

Previous pages: Wine royalty: like father like son, Alexis Lichine and Sacha Lichine.
Above: Sacha Lichine, the rosé pioneer of Provence.

Born in Bordeaux but primarily raised and educated in New York and Boston, Sacha returned to the family business only after having worked the full spectrum of roles in the wine world. He slapped labels on bottles, led wine tours for affluent oenophiles, worked as a sommelier at the now-shuttered Anthony's Pier 4 in Boston, worked for the major US distributor Southern Glazer's Wines & Spirits, and produced wine in Burgundy, Bordeaux, and the Languedoc. By the time he inherited a struggling Prieuré-Lichine from his father in 1987, two years before his death, Sacha was already becoming a household name in his own right.

Owing to these experiences, Sacha was primed to build something of his own. It was less a question of *if* than of *when*. He had first visited Château d'Esclans in 1994, when it had been up for sale. At the time, he was working to get the Prieuré back on track but kept his eye on other high-potential regions. It wasn't so much the prospect of overhauling the estate, then in great disrepair, that stopped him from getting out his checkbook then and there, it was the global rosé market's lack of readiness and his obligations back in Bordeaux. He was both strapped for resources and unconvinced of the timing.

"I knew that there was something to be done with Côtes de Provence wines, but it was too soon, and it was going to be too costly," Sacha recalls. "I thought, it's not going to work now." He paused the idea of a big move and ran the Prieuré until he sold it in 1999, partially to pay off his father's debts. But the decision was also about being free to begin a new chapter and forge his own path—one that would take him away from Bordeaux, away from the region's inconsistent vintages and fierce competition, and most importantly, away from his father's mark.

In the decade following the sale, Sacha returned frequently to Provence to keep tabs on Château d'Esclans. In 1995, the Château had been purchased by a Swedish pension fund that had allowed the wine operation to all but wither. He ramped up visits to other estates in the region, considering some thirty-two properties, but his mind kept returning to Esclans, with its Tuscan-style farmhouse and eighty-year-old grenache vines full of vibrant life.

"I remember visiting Sacha in 2000. He had recently sold the Prieuré and was renting a place in Ramatuelle. I was riding on the back of a Vespa with him when he stopped suddenly, cocks the heel of his right foot to stabilize it, and looks down in the direction of the Esclans Valley," begins Tom Schreckinger, Château d'Esclans's director of communication. "He waved his hands around wildly and announced, 'One day, I'm going to own a rosé vineyard down there.' I said, 'You just sold the Prieuré, do you really want to jump from the frying pan back into the fire?' Of course, he did."

In 2005, the opportunity presented itself again; only this time, the moment was right. The acquisition of Château d'Esclans was complete one year later and would inspire his boldest ambition yet: upending the maligned reputation of rosé by producing the best and most rarefied wine of its kind in the world.

Opposite: From the archives: Château d'Esclans changed hands several times in the nineteenth and twentieth centuries. One previous owner, Joseph Toussaint Caussemille, transformed its architecture into the Tuscan-style Sacha Lichine fell in love with. **Following pages:** Long before Sacha Lichine brought the Château back to life, it was occupied by various owners, nobles and others, and had fallen into disrepair. The canvas was ready for a transformation.

"I WOULD HAVE NEVER BEEN ABLE TO PURSUE THIS IF THERE WEREN'T A PROPERTY, AN ANCHOR, TO GIVE IT LEGITIMACY. THERE'S ANCIENT VINES, REAL TERROIR, REAL HISTORY. IT'S A MAGICAL PLACE."

Sacha Lichine

Previous pages: Picture-perfect blue hydrangeas in full bloom at Château d'Esclans.
Opposite: Magnificent blue hydrangeas line the path to Sacha Lichine's Tuscan-style farmhouse.

Previous pages: Wintry Provençal glow at Château d'Esclans.
Above: The legendary Provençal luminosity that brings life to Château d'Esclans,
even in the depths of winter. **Opposite:** Inside the Esclans chapel, where two cherubic
angels perched over the altar appear to be whispering to one another.

For all its Provençal charm and hints of Tuscany, the Château itself was in a dire state when Sacha took over. It required a dramatic decorative facelift to make it suitable not only as a family home but also as a veritable destination for friends, VIPs, and oenophiles to discover the plenitude of his pale-pink elixirs.

In the long history of the Château and wine estate within the Terres d'Esclans, the broader land on which they sit, it was first the Comtes de Provence who inherited ownership (already controlling much of the region) in the early twelfth century before bestowing the estate in 1200 to the noble Villeneuve family from Marseille. The Villeneuves maintained ownership up until the early eighteenth century, at which point they began gradually selling off lots, first because of marriages and family successions but then as a political fallout of the French Revolution, which left them impoverished like most of the families descended from the nobility of the Middle Ages. As a result, the Château was left separated from two other neighboring estates, the Domaine des Grands Esclans and the Domaine du Jas d'Esclans.

Château d'Esclans changed hands several times in the nineteenth and twentieth centuries, initially, and perhaps most importantly, with Joseph Toussaint Caussemille. Caussemille was responsible for transforming the architecture of the Château—removing the original dungeon and restoring the roof and facade in Tuscan style. It was this elegant structure that Sacha Lichine would later discover, owned by the Swedish pension fund, and overhaul from top to bottom.

Previous pages: The angels that inspired a legend—Whispering Angel.
Opposite: A family affair: Sacha Lichine and his wife, Mathilde, led the redesign of Château d'Esclans, where they live part of the year with their five children. **Following pages:** The fumoir in the Lichine Château lends an elegant backdrop to insouciant afternoons among wine lovers.

The Sacha Lichine iteration of the Château d'Esclans estate sits nestled in the Esclans Valley in France's Var department on a lush swath of land that has evolved with their production needs to include 267 hectares of planted vines of primarily grenache and rolle (vermentino). Ruins of an old watchtower, once a lookout point to spot intruders weaving their way into the gulf of Fréjus, sit atop the massif that overlooks the Château; another medieval vestige, the twelfth-century cellar is a reminder of the land's 2,500-year-old history that Sacha and his company preserve.

Today, guests arriving at the estate are greeted by international flags waving gently above the entrance, a clear sign of a global outlook. Soaring plane trees, whispering as they sway, and rows of blue hydrangeas usher visitors in further, while the cicadas' signature serenade lends an unmistakable sense of place. The scene resembles nothing short of a painting fit for museum walls and yet every picturesque inch of Château d'Esclans is not just visually enchanting, it is essential to the house's viticultural innovation.

Opposite: The family legacy guest books sit on the drawing room's desk.
Following pages: The drawing room, brimming with family photographs and iconic wine books.

F rom this remote perch, just far enough away from the energy of Nice, the festive vibes of Saint-Tropez, and the jet-setters of Monaco, Sacha Lichine built and developed a brand that would grow to become a fixture in the most illustrious homes, bars, hotels, and restaurants in all three locales, in addition to a cornerstone of the most alluring destinations around the world.

In the process, he has also reunited the trifecta of estates that composed the historic majority of Terres d'Esclans, having acquired the Domaines des Grands Esclans in 2020 and the Domaine du Jas d'Esclans in 2023. Overall, these acquisitions brought the total and current land holdings to nearly 610 hectares. It can now be said that Sacha Lichine and his brand extend over nearly the entirety of the prestigious wine-growing Esclans valley.

Still, Lichine holds particular affection for Château d'Esclans, the birthplace of his rosé vision. "It's a magical place. I would have never been able to pursue this if there weren't a property, an anchor, to give it legitimacy," Sacha says. "There's ancient vines, real terroir, real soil, real history. But we can't bottle *exactly* what happens here." That may be true but he and his team certainly come very close.

Previous pages: One of several dining rooms at the Château that welcomes VIP guests and friends of the house. **Opposite:** A glimpse of the Château kitchen, where the most elegant of feasts are prepared for Sacha Lichine's most prized guests. **Following pages:** An evening of learning and entertainment. Special guests from across the world come to Château d'Esclans to discover viticulture and winemaking methods. The valley in all its glory.

BRINGING ROSÉ TO LIFE

"THE OLDER THE VINE, THE MORE INTERESTING THE FRUIT"
SACHA LICHINE SAYS.

Wine fridges may have long been spoken for by sparkling and white wines, but judging by the soaring success of rosé Champagne, Sacha knew there was room—both physically and economically—for a still rosé. He wouldn't consider himself clairvoyant, merely entrenched enough in the business to push boundaries. "In England fifteen years ago or so, I noticed that women were drinking a lot of rosé Champagne. They loved it because of the beautiful blush-pink color, the invigorating effervescence, and even the glass it was served in. They could sip it and be reminded of their holidays on the Côte d'Azur."

Among his deepest beliefs was that as long as the product was flawless, he could turn rosé into the Champagne of still wines which would earn the respect of discerning wine drinkers.

Such ambition required an all-star team, a precise technical vision, and the means to make it happen. Key to the venture was Patrick Léon, the esteemed oenologist from Bordeaux who, like Sacha Lichine, was a relative Provence outsider. Léon had begun his career in 1972 alongside Alexis Lichine in Bordeaux and was freshly retired from his role as technical director at Baron Philippe de Rothschild when Sacha tapped him to lend his acclaimed technical expertise to the project.

Opposite: The hilly slopes of the westernmost vineyards on an early winter morning.
Following pages: A dusting of wintry snow on Château d'Esclans.

"Patrick Léon was the best of the best. I trusted him implicitly, even if he initially disagreed with the taste profile I wanted for these wines. He would've made something darker and juicier," explains Lichine. As Patrick's son, Bertrand Léon, technical director of Château d'Esclans since 2011, tells it today, "The idea was, and still is, to make wines with weight and freshness. If you take Whispering Angel, for example, it's a classic expression of rosé de Provence, where we evoke density but highlight aromatic freshness."

In other words, Sacha and Patrick ultimately found common ground, agreeing to focus on producing a line of wines that they would not only love to drink themselves but would also stick it to the naysayers in the French wine establishment for whom rosé was dismissed as a faux wine, the Coca-Cola of wine, as some went so far as to say. Time would prove them wrong.

Opposite: The Château d'Esclans vines, some of which are close to hundred years old, are an integral part of the legacy that drew Sacha Lichine to this land.
Following pages: Winter's conclusion in the vines.

Above and opposite: Signs of spring at Château d'Esclans.
Following pages: The vibrant, early green of the vines in their six-month maturation cycle.

"OF COURSE,
EVERYONE THOUGHT
I WAS CRAZY. IT WAS
AN ENORMOUS RISK.
BUT WHERE THERE ARE
NO RISKS, THERE ARE
NO REWARDS."

Sacha Lichine

Previous page, above and opposite: The grape as it matures gradually.
Following pages: Summer arrives in all its vibrant glory to the vines of Château d'Esclans.

Shifting rosé's reputation from a cheap and cheerful pool wine to one on par with sophisticated red and white fine wines was going to require heavy technical lifting. "Rosé is the hardest wine to produce—well," Sacha and Bertrand often say. Particularly when the goal is making Burgundian-style rosé and especially when the land has nearly thirty different types of soil and several grapes varieties. For Bertrand, "making high-quality rosé requires specialized equipment and innovative technical capabilities."

Fortunately, they were prepared to do what no other rosé producer in Provence had pursued before.

The estate, part of which is dominated by nearly hundred-year-old grenache vines that yield a high concentration of flavor, is divided into two subregions: Due south of the Château, Fréjus is flat with high sun exposure and soil rich in clay that is most suitable for younger vines. The more elevated parcels in the foothills of Draguignan, the second subregion, feature older grenache vines used to make the house's top-end cuvées (Les Clans and Garrus, see pages 141 and 143). There, the roots of the oldest vines stretch deep into the chalk and rocky limestone soil, exposing the vines to different stratas of minerality.

Opposite: The end of summer signals the crucial moment for the coming year: the harvest can commence. **Following pages:** An intergenerational group of pickers from nearby villages descends on the vines at sunrise to begin a half day of intense work.

Opposite: Sunrise to noon amid the vines is the grape-picker's routine throughout the harvest in the late weeks of summer. **Above:** Ready to be picked. Sacha and Bertrand often say that rosé is a difficult wine to produce well, particularly when the goal is making Burgundian-style rosé and especially when the land has nearly thirty different types of soil and several grapes varieties.

B eyond understanding this unique terroir and adapting accordingly, technical prowess comes down to how the grapes are harvested, vinified, and reared.

The methods Patrick Léon first put into place in 2006 reflect first-growth standards and begin with harvesting the grapes by hand. Each year in the last weeks of summer, an intergenerational group of pickers residing in nearby villages descends on the vines at sunrise while the grapes are still cool from the previous night. They work tirelessly, cheering each other on as they fill their ten-kilogram crates to the brim, but only until noon. At this point, the heat becomes far too great—both for them and the grapes—to continue.

Large trucks then deposit the grapes to the cellar where a team manually sorts them. With swift, fluid movements they pluck out unwanted objects—leaves and twigs, and any obviously unripe or damaged grapes—before the bunch passes on to optical sorting. The machine discards any subpar grapes that don't match the benchmark shape, size, and color established by the cellar master, Jean-Claude Neu.

Opposite: The pickers begin their work early in the day, fillling their quotas before the heat of the sun forces work to stop at noon.

The grapes continue on after picking and sorting to be cooled and pressed. It is here that Sacha Lichine and Patrick Léon have set up one of the most noteworthy innovations of their operation: a wide-reaching system of temperature control. The grapes are sent through a soft-crush mechanism that allows the juice inside to flow. Next, the grapes enter a heat exchange system in double-layered stainless steel pipes that reduce the temperature from as high as 25°C (77°F) to as low as 7 to 8°C (45° to 46°F), which ensures that freshness and vigor are locked in place. This reduced temperature is especially important to prepare the grapes for a closed-loop press that makes use of giant bags of inert gas filled with nitrogen to prevent oxidation during the pressing process while also preserving the aromatic qualities of the grapes.

The press yields three grades of primarily free-run juice that passes next through *débourbage*, or degumming. This is the process of settling the freshly pressed grape must by gravity, allowing undesirable solids to tumble to the bottom of the vat. This step is essential prior to fermentation and ensures the technical team can achieve the desired characteristics: clean, pale and clear wine.

Previous pages and opposite: Throughout the harvest, a team manually sorts the grapes picked that morning, plucking out unwanted objects, such as leaves and twigs. **Following pages:** Coming together is as fundamental to the harvest as the grape-picking ritual itself. During the harvest, pickers lunch together daily at Château d'Esclans.

Opposite and above: Autumnal transformation as the vines turn completely red.
Following pages: The warmth of autumn at Château d'Esclans as the vinyeards fade into
deep yellows, reds, and oranges.

Depending on the grade of juice produced in the pressing process, Bertrand Léon and Jean-Claude Neu determine the most suitable fermentation method: stainless steel tanks, oak barrels, or a combination of both. For Whispering Angel, the house's flagship wine (perhaps better known as the most sold French rosé in the world), 100 percent of the grapes are vinified in temperature-controlled stainless steel tanks. However, for its most innovative cru wines, Les Clans and Garrus, the grapes are entirely fermented and reared up to eleven months in six-hundred-liter, individually temperature-controlled, semi-toasted oak barrels (called *demi-muids*) from Bordeaux and Burgundy. During this time, they undergo *bâtonnage*, the process of stirring the lees (settled sediment) back into the wine, twice weekly, which Sacha insists allows them to create rosés that can be kept up to a decade.

This Burgundian vision of vinification, initiated by Patrick Léon and evolved further by Bertrand, was considered radical when the house put their first four cuvées on the market in 2006. "Generally, rosé in Provence is vinified through stainless steel or cement vats, which is what we do for Whispering Angel and Rock Angel. But to barrel-rear the others, partially or fully, is both a tremendous investment and a way to achieve a completely different flavor profile than whatever existed for rosé," explains Bertrand Léon, adding that they switch out the oak barrels after three years, when the oaky flavor imparted on the wine has become less strong. If the use of oak began as somewhat of an experiment for the first vintage, it has become conviction, a choice that lends greater depth, complexity, and a rounder mouthfeel to the wine.

Opposite: Cellar master Jean-Claude Neu taste-testing the juice being vinified in individually temperature-controlled, semi-toasted oak barrels. **Following pages:** The oak barrels in which the house's innovative cru wines, Les Clans and Garrus, are completely fermented and reared. Rock Angel and Château d'Esclans juices are partially fermented and reared in them.

"TWENTY-FIVE YEARS AGO, WE WOULDN'T HAVE BEEN ABLE TO MAKE ROSÉ THIS WAY BECAUSE THE TECHNOLOGY SIMPLY DIDN'T EXIST."

Sacha Lichine

Opposite: Château d'Esclans rosés are partially or fully vinified in oak barrels rather than stainless steel or cement vats like most Provençal rosés. This technique was established by Patrick Léon, the Château's founding consulting oenologist, and continued by Bertrand Léon, his son, who is currently the technical director. This yields a radically different flavor profile than what has historically existed for rosé.

More than fifteen years after its pioneering debut as the finest and most expensive rosé in the world (more than one hundred dollars per bottle), it's no wonder that Garrus has often been compared to an elegant white Burgundy. The highly prized wine was once sipped by the late Queen Elizabeth II and a host of other dignitaries at a charity dinner; today, it regularly finds itself on the tables of the "happy few," everywhere from Singapore to Buenos Aires.

The premium focus may have been a risk that generated more than a few skeptics at its start, but the industry's most discerning palates have unanimously rallied around the collection of rosés year after year, convinced of their merit.

Ultimately, it's the signature Lichine alchemy of quality, vision, and technical excellence that paved the way for an entirely new category of fine pink wines—with the Château d'Esclans portfolio leading the charge.

Opposite, from top to bottom and left to right:
Franck Fantino, vineyard manager; Bertrand Léon, technical director,
with Jean-Claude Neu, cellar master, Sacha Lichine and Patrick Léon, founding consulting
oenologist; Shannon Benoist, head of sales and logistic administration; Alan Wong, Asia manager;
Clément Malochet, French brand ambassador; Tom Schreckinger, communications director;
Sacha Lichine and his son, Alexis Lichine; Alain Rivière, global sales director
and Paul Chevalier, North American vice president and global marketing director.

Following page, from top to bottom and left to right:
Patrick Léon; setting up a private tasting at the Château; bottles lined up for a private tasting;
Sacha Lichine tastes the blending of the wines; Robert Reiplinger, general manager;
wine-making team at the blending of the wines; blended wines arranged for tasting.

"*WE CREATED A PHENOMENON IN PROVENCE, SOMETHING THAT TRULY HADN'T BEEN DONE BEFORE.*"

Sacha Lichine

Following pages: The rosés (left to right): Whispering Angel,
The Beach, Château d'Esclans, The Pale, Rock Angel. A rosy setting sun on Château d'Esclans,
just as the evening arrives, and abundant glasses of Les Clans and Garrus are served.

THE WINES

ACCORDING TO SACHA LICHINE, "WINE SHOUD BE TAKEN SIMPLY. EITHER IT GIVES YOU PLEASURE OR IT DOESN'T. YOU MUST BELIEVE IN YOUR TASTE."

GARRUS

Superior is the operative word when it comes to Garrus, the house's *tête de cuvée*. Meant for a fine wine, the grapes are primarily selected from the most treasured single parcel within the vineyards of Château d'Esclans. The parcel boasts a high concentration of nearly hundred-year-old, low-yielding grenache vines. Garrus is the most complex expression of Côtes de Provence, composed of grenache grapes that are blended with a touch of rolle (vermentino), 90 percent free-run juice, vinified exclusively in six-hundred-liter temperature-controlled new and second-year oak barrels (demi-muids) during which bâtonnage is conducted twice weekly over an eleven-month period prior to bottling.

Garrus is known for its fruity depth, bright acidity and powerful mouthfeel, with subtle notes of oak, luscious red fruit, and a creamy texture. For its stunning level of quality and pioneering vinification, Garrus was unveiled to the market as the most expensive and luxurious rosé ever produced. Wine critic Roger Voss proclaimed that "this wine takes the concept of Provence rosé to the extreme"—but in the best way possible.

LES CLANS

The captivating sibling to Garrus, Les Clans has established itself as an important wine with great structure and understated elegance that offers a more complex take on Provençal rosé. Made from a blend of largely old-vine grenache and rolle and 90 percent free-run juice, the wine is reared ten months in new and second-year demi-muids and undergoes bâtonnage twice weekly.

Alluring woody, vanilla, and fresh fruits notes develop on the nose and give way to a refreshing but rich and satiny, barely there oak texture on the palate. Medium-bodied, the cuvée has just the right amount of quintessential summer rosé freshness and minerality to balance a lengthy, saline finish. Take it from the esteemed wine author Jane Anson, who praised Les Clans as "a serious wine that still has the fresh lightness of touch of a perfect summer rosé, it's understated but always utterly more-ish."

CHÂTEAU D'ESCLANS

The first of three premium rosés, there's a reason the namesake cuvée is considered the soul of the estate. It is 100 percent estate grown and bottled, made exclusively from grenache and rolle sourced from Château d'Esclans vineyards. A mix of free-run juice and first slight pressing (but no maceration), this classic wine brings together different technical approaches, undergoing fermentation in both stainless steel and oak barrels to give it a harmonious combination of freshness and complexity.

This cuvée is a medium-bodied rosé with a sophisticated nose dominated by floral and red-berry fruit notes alongside a touch of vanilla and pear. It delivers a smooth, creamy texture that is rich and long on the palate, and a substantial saline finish that makes it elegantly expressive.

WHISPERING ANGEL

I t all started with a whisper. The flagship cuvée of Caves d'Esclans and the world's reference for dry rosés owes its name to the cherubic angels perched above the altar in the Château d'Esclans chapel who appear to be whispering to one another. In selecting these two unassuming but evocative words, Sacha did what no other Provençal producer had done before: he made rosé inclusive and, to a degree, culturally agnostic. "English is the great equalizer, far easier to pronounce," believes Sacha. That was particularly important considering that most of the Provençal rosés on the market at the time of Whispering Angel's launch were more intent on playing up the aura of the region or a French name than working to make their wines better. Any chance he gets, Sacha reiterates that "if Whispering Angel wasn't as good as it is, it wouldn't sell. It's all about what goes into the bottle, not a name. At the end of the day, it's what sells the product and keeps people coming back for more."

Elegantly pale, fresh, and marvelously fruit-forward, this best-in-class rosé (and a favorite among everyone from the discerning rosé lover to famous figures like Adele) is the most accessible and uncomplicated of the house's original four cuvées. A blend of free-run and pressed juices from grenache, cinsault, and rolle grapes sourced from the Esclans Valley and the Côte de Provence region's choice vineyards, the finely aromatic, bone-dry wine with a smooth finish is 100 percent fermented and reared in stainless steel tanks with precise temperature control. A classic expression of rosé de Provence, Whispering Angel paved the way for the premium, more nuanced wines in the portfolio and inspired a rosé renaissance.

ROCK ANGEL

First the angels whispered, then they came to rock. Bright and consistent with a more rounded structure and mouthfeel than Whispering Angel, Rock Angel is a character-rich cuvée from Caves d'Esclans. This wine is a blend of grenache, cinsault, and rolle sourced from grapes primarily from Château d'Esclans vineyards as well as the choicest parcels in the vicinity of the Esclans Valley and the nearby the Côtes de Provence region. A mix of free-run and gently pressed juices, Rock Angel is partially vinified in six-hundred-liter oak casks (demi-muids) as well as temperature-controlled stainless steel tanks, during which bâtonnage is conducted twice weekly over a six-month period prior to bottling.

Rock Angel consistently delivers complex aromas which elevates the wine to a more premium realm but remains easy to drink—so much so it lends itself beautifully both to casual aperitif hours and food-driven experiences. Those fond of the minerality in a glass of Sancerre find their ideal rosé match in Rock Angel.

THE BEACH

Where there was still further opportunity for Sacha and company was in the entry-level segment. Priced less than twenty dollars per bottle, The Beach (which replaced The Palm) and The Pale, the most recent additions to the portfolio, speak to the young, upwardly mobile but still a bit budget-conscious consumer who wants an easier, more accessible way into the aspirational rosé lifestyle. These easy-to-sip wines are meant for newer drinkers to the category who may get easily lost in a sea of lower-priced, candy-flavored rosés. "These wines educate the younger generation about the work that goes into making rosé, about what rosé is and should be. It's about leading them in the right direction and eventually providing a bridge to Whispering Angel and our premium wines," says Paul Chevalier.

Ideal for casual, unpretentious gatherings, The Beach blends the grenache, cinsault, and syrah grapes sourced from top-choice vineyards in the appellation of Côteaux d'Aix-en-Provence and is vinified in temperature-controlled stainless steel tanks.

From the very first pour, it's clear: The Beach is a playful and refreshing wine with great aromatic freshness on the nose, including aromas of red berries and hints of lime and melon. On the palate, it demonstrates balanced acidity and minerality with citrus and red fruit flavors that finish fresh and round. As an ode to seaside culture and idyllic coastlines, the wine also reflects a commitment to preservation: not only through a partnership with the Surfrider Foundation, which encompasses coast-to-coast beach cleanups, special gatherings, and donations, but through packaging. The lighter glass bottle requires less energy to produce and decreases the carbon footprint of heavy shipping loads, while the recyclable screw cap makes it easier to open in outdoor spaces.

THE PALE

The Pale, with its playful label evoking glamorous Roaring Twenties soirée scenes in the spirit of a *New Yorker* magazine cover and its chic bottle with a fluted base, brings this wine into a sophisticated cocktail party register. The name is a nod to the English expression, "Who's for a glass of the pale?" Redolent of a *vin gris*, the wine is a blend of grenache, rolle, syrah, and cinsault sourced from the most choice vineyards in Vin de Pays in the Var region. The mix of softly pressed juices are left on their lees in stainless steel tanks for five to eight months to lend a creamy texture to a quintessential bone-dry rosé. Expressive inside and out, The Pale delivers subtle fruit notes. Matthew Jukes calls it "a cross between a tangy white and a sultry rosé" that is as seductive to look at as it is to drink.

GETTING IT
OFF THE GROUND

THERE'S A NATURAL TENDENCY TO TRY AND PARSE BRANDS AND THE PEOPLE WHO CREATE THEM INTO CATCHY ONE-LINERS, BUT CHÂTEAU D'ESCLANS AND SACHA LICHINE ESCAPE THAT CATEGORIZATION. THERE MAY HAVE BEEN A CONSPICUOUS OPPORTUNITY IN THE ROSÉ MARKET BUT NOT JUST ANYONE COULD ELEVATE IT TO ONE WORTHY OF THE WORLD'S ICONIC FINE WINES. NOR COULD IT HAVE BEEN DONE WITHOUT THE RIGHT TEAM, STORY, OR DISTRIBUTION STRATEGY. AND THAT DOESN'T FIT NEATLY INTO A TAGLINE.

A t the core of this venture remains quality, the crucial element without which it never would have lifted off the vines. In fact, Lichine and his acolytes rhapsodize so freely about quality that it has become something of a Château d'Esclans signature. In truth, it's this obsession with quality that raised the bar for the entire region. "Part of the reason the category has become what it is today is because the prices are higher. When we arrived here, we were paying 80 euros per hectoliter of grapes and finished wine. Now it's more than 300 euros. The smartest growers put the money they make back into constantly improving the quality."

Still, to thrive in wine the way that Sacha Lichine has requires more than a quality product, it requires vision—how to sell it, how to get it into glasses, and how to maintain it year on year. With his Bordeaux bonafides, Lichine brought the ultimate winemaking toolkit to Provence, putting him ahead of the game. "The trend in Provence was to focus on beautiful labels and names, on making the wine (even if it wasn't good enough). But most producers hadn't mastered distribution," Lichine explains. "Success means understanding the wine business, how to produce quality wine, *and* how to distribute it. That was my background so right out of the gate, I had a leg up."

As he tells it, the texture of the distribution tale was one of rolling-up-the-sleeves hard work. It's the spirit of a start-up mixed with the old-world knowledge of a traveling salesman. He calls it the Estée Lauder approach: visiting every single venue and hot spot, in every single city that mattered, and getting the wines tasted by the people who mattered, a technique that's not so far off from the "shake hands, make friends, sell wines" method his father swore by. Sacha deeply understood that the pursuit of excellence would only matter if he and his team could get the product in front of the most influential gatekeepers—wine directors for bars and restaurants, club owners, hotel groups, bartenders, and if he were lucky, sommeliers.

Previous pages: The majestic views of the Massif des Maures and the Rocher de Roquebrune from the Château d'Esclans terrace. **Opposite:** The Château d'Esclans crest, a gauge of quality. The orange hue to the rosé develops naturally in larger bottles and with time and maturation.

LES CLANS

Château D'ESCLANS
DOMAINES SACHA LICHINE

LES CLANS

Château D'ESCLANS
DOMAINES SACHA LICHINE

"The consumer rarely arrives at a restaurant, bar or even wine shop knowing what they want. How many times have you gone to a store and had the salesperson say, Try this one, not this one? They're the ones who say, Yes, I'll take a case. They're the ones selling it. But with sommeliers, most of the time they make you drink what they want you to drink. And you'll never end up drinking what you want to drink," Sacha explains. The wine seller and the bartender, first and foremost, played instrumental roles in getting Whispering Angel in front of clients. "In the beginning, a lot of people didn't know much about wines and would be offered a glass of rosé to which they would say, Oh no that's too sweet, and the bartender would tell them about these new rosés from Provence that are dry, that they're going to love. It's like a rosé Champagne. If the bartender recommends it, you listen."

But to persuade them, Sacha needed to pack his suitcases full of bottles and hit the ground running.

"It wasn't going to happen by bringing people to the Château (although people would come years later). We were out on the streets, putting it into their mouths. I know Americans in the wine business. I know that even those who have never been to Europe can tell you about every single appellation in Burgundy, Bordeaux, and the Rhône, subregions in Germany and Italy, because they've drunk the wine and educated themselves," he says. "You can't expect them to come to you, no matter how much great press you get or how beautiful your estate is. You must go to them." With years of experience from vine to bottle, Sacha knew exactly who to approach.

Previous pages: Les Clans, ready to be taken home.
Opposite: Pop it open and let the wine speak for itself. That's how Sacha Lichine put rosé on the map, one glass and one bottle of Whispering Angel at a time. **Following pages:** The elevated, exceptional land on which the rosé renaissance was born.

"These wine directors and bartenders are always looking for something new. You have to convince the buyers. I had to convince the food and beverage manager at the Mandarin Oriental in Hong Kong that he should believe in my idea of what rosé could be," recounts Sacha. "And the only way I could do that was by presenting them with a legitimately good glass of wine."

That doesn't mean it was easy. Paul Chevalier, one of the original five in the team who oversees the brand's development in North America as vice president, distinctly remembers going up against detractors. "It took us a good six or seven years to take off. Initially, when we'd show up to get decision-makers to try the wine, we were treated like the inferior beings of the wine business."

A salesman at heart, Sacha didn't let the occasional insult keep him from trying because he knew that once they tasted his wine, the deal was sealed. "In Chicago, I remember going to see seller after seller and they all said they didn't drink rosé there, it was too low-end, too cheap. Then, they balked at the price of Garrus. After the first sip, they ordered several cases. That's how I opened more than a hundred accounts in only a few days."

Opposite: From lunch to dinner, no matter where or when one drinks it, Whispering Angel is the perfect touch of Provence.

After living for a time in Chicago to be close to retailers and tastemakers, Sacha made Hong Kong, and later Singapore, his home base to develop the relationships needed to get his wines into all the best places— a geographic and economic investment few winemakers are prepared to make.

From there, the proverbial snowball effect worked its magic, amplified by the story of the Château and Sacha's unexpected mix of American work ethic and French love of the land. Once winemakers saw the success of Whispering Angel and the premium cuvées, they too wanted to make better rosé and tap into the market. "But they didn't know how to do it or have the right process or the mindset or really know the way to go to market," says Chevalier. "We manage our key accounts directly— we know them personally. We've always run a different operation to most other domaines. And we have a story. Alexis Lichine educated Americans about wine. We're educating people about rosé."

The critical success of the Château d'Esclans portfolio may have come from convincing the toughest wine critics but the commercial success came from relationship building, superb storytelling and, as the old adage goes, location, location, location.

Opposite: Elegantly pale, fresh, and marvelously fruit-forward, Whispering Angel inspired a rosé renaissance.

f Provence is the historic heart of the operation, it is across the United States and nearby Caribbean that birthed the brand's tentacular reach.

As the flagship cuvée, Whispering Angel needed to be in all the best places, where the beau monde in every city not only goes to be seen but wants to be seen consuming the very best. These are the kinds of iconic destinations with international crowds that Sacha frequented himself—the Four Seasons in Chicago, The Beverly Hills Hotel, Fontainebleau Miami Beach, Mick Jagger's properties on Mustique, Eden Rock on St. Barths, and the hubs of American sophistication and high society, Nantucket, Martha's Vineyard, and the Hamptons.

Sacha was set on these distribution points because he knew, perhaps better than anyone else in Provence, who his end client would be and where they spent their time. And he was certain they were going to love his wines because it would be on offer wherever they traveled. "That's what makes it chic—it's because the wine is in the right places—a mix of historical and iconic destinations," explains Sacha. "They begin to associate our brand with those locales. And as people migrate seasonally, we follow them. Where they go, we go." Lichine rosés followed the crowds to the finest ski slopes in Aspen, St. Moritz, and Gstaad to be the gold standard of après-ski. And they followed them to their far-flung getaways in Phuket, Hong Kong, and Singapore.

Opposite, from top to bottom and left to right:
The destinations that birthed Whispering Angel's reach: Hôtel du Cap-Eden-Roc, Antibes, France; Atlantis The Royal, Dubai, United Arab Emirates; La Guérite, Cannes, France; The Fontainebleau, Miami, Florida, US; The Beverly Hills Hotel, Los Angeles, California, US; Rock House, Turks and Caicos.

Following pages, from top to bottom and left to right:
Cotton House, Mustique, Saint Vincent and Grenadines; Nikki Beach, Gustavia, St. Barths; Four Seasons Resort The Ocean Club, Nassau, Bahamas; Four Seasons Resort Nevis, Charlestown, Saint Kitts and Nevis; Catch Beach Club, Phuket, Thailand; Cheval Blanc, St. Barths; Bagatelle, Tulum, Mexico; Sandy Lane, Saint James, Barbados; Nammos, Mykonos, Greece.

On the long journey to making Whispering Angel (and, subsequently, the premium cuvées) a fixture of any top-shelf wine list or aspirational destination, there were, of course, pivotal moments that moved the dial. Paul Chevalier points to 2012, when The Delano in Miami put Whispering Angel on the menu by the glass and when the SoHo House rooftop bar started pouring it a year later. He highlights the Chiltern Firehouse and Annabel's in London adding the wine to their offering by the glass as important shifts, sending the message that "it was the cool rosé for the cool people."

He calls out the first of an annual author's night event in the Hamptons he was involved with as decisive in associating Whispering Angel with the literary elite. And with each successive cultural partnership, from Coachella to Art Basel, the enduring buzz around Whispering Angel secured the brand an even broader drinking audience. "Because the wine is in the right places, with the David Beckhams, Gigi Hadids, and Martha Stewarts of the world, you convert them and everyone else to your product organically," says Chevalier. "They became our de facto ambassadors, entertaining guests with our wines and sharing them on social media for the world to see."

Previous pages: Whispering Angel dresses up every occasion. It was served in every glass at the Goodwood Horse Racing Festival (shown here) in Chichester, UK.

Opposite, from top to bottom and left to right:
Hotel Cipriani, Venice, Italy; Chiltern Firehouse, London, UK; The Dempsey Cookhouse and Bar, Singapore; Annabel's, London, UK; The Peninsula, Paris, France; Marina Bay Sands, Singapore.

"*THE CONSUMER RARELY ARRIVES AT A RESTAURANT, BAR OR EVEN WINE SHOP KNOWING WHAT THEY WANT. HOW MANY TIMES HAVE YOU GONE TO A STORE AND HAD THE SALESPERSON SAY, TRY THIS ONE, NOT THIS ONE? THEY ARE THE PEOPLE SELLING IT.*"

Sacha Lichine

As with any winning formula, all the variables have to align for a brand to reach cult status. In this case, the pale pink color was not only attractive, but it instantly distinguished Château d'Esclans and Caves d'Esclans wines from the deep salmony rosés of yesteryear. Beyond its obvious elegance, the pale hue conveys the dry Provençal style that few consumers even knew was possible to achieve with a rosé before Lichine came along. "Typically, the lighter the rosé, the dryer it will taste," explains Lichine, adding that it's also an indication of the house's approach—short maceration or very little grape skin contact. "Darker pink rosés lean sweeter. So, the paler the better, in my opinion."

Color also plays a role right down to the bottle itself. "Aside from Sauterne, rosé is the only wine to come in a clear glass bottle. Before you even pour it, you can imagine what the wine will look like in your glass," says Sacha. "Consumers were looking for something festive, for something new to associate themselves with. Color adds to the wine's overall image as chicer than the rest."

Opposite, from top to bottom and left to right:
Hakkasan Mayfair, London, UK; SEVVA, Hong Kong, China; Mandarin Oriental, Bangkok, Thailand; Juvia, Miami, Florida, US; LPM, Abu Dhabi, United Arab Emirates; SoHo House, New York, US; China Club, Hong Kong, China; The Peninsula, Hong Kong, China.

In the early days this was especially true for women, whom Lichine credits with having catapulted his portfolio to greatness: English women who regularly popped over to the Côte d'Azur, like at the Hôtel du Cap-Eden-Roc in Antibes for a long weekend and returned home bearing more than a few bottles, as well as the quintessential coastal American who summered on Nantucket or the Hamptons. Women who often reached for Veuve Clicquot one night, Cloudy Bay Sauvignon Blanc the next, and a bottle of rosé on another. Women who told their friends, who told their friends, and who, one by one, propelled the brand's success through word-of-mouth.

While rosé's syrupy-sweet reputation may have long reduced it to the drink of choice among wine novices, Sacha's winemaking pedigree disrupted the idea once and for all. His wines weren't gendered, they were for every kind of consumer, at all stages of their lives. "It's not just water with a little alcohol and a pink color, it's REAL wine. That's why when Patrick Léon came on board and asked what our big idea was going to be, I said, 'We're going to make real, drinkable wine'."

It's precisely those eminently drinkable, sophisticated, dry wines with the most desirable sultry pale pink tint that informed if not a revolution, then a veritable lifestyle.

Opposite, from top to bottom and left to right:
Nobu Hotel, Ibiza Bay, Spain; Bürgenstock Resort, Obbürgen, Switzerland; Hotel Splendido, Portofino, Italy; Puente Romano Beach Resort, Marbella, Spain; La Mamounia, Marrakesh, Morocco; Rialto Restaurant, Gstaad, Switzerland.

A ROSY
STATE OF MIND

IT MAY HAVE REQUIRED AN IMAGINATIVE LEAP TO BELIEVE THAT
SACHA LICHINE WOULD PULL OFF THE WHOLESALE REINVEN-
TION OF ROSÉ, BUT NOT EVEN LICHINE HIMSELF COULD HAVE
ANTICIPATED THE EXTENT TO WHICH THE CONSUMER WOULD
ELEVATE HIS STYLE OF ROSÉ TO MORE THAN A WINE BUT TO
A STATE OF MIND.

Previous pages: An early evening celebration at Château d'Esclans begins by taking in the view. Sacha Lichine, always the ultimate host: A VIP reception at Château d'Esclans. Sacha, Mathilde and their son, Alexis, pose on the staircase in front of the Château. On the right, Sashka and Margaux, Sacha and Mathilde's daughters. At the bottom right, Tom Schreckinger with some guests.

Previous pages: The night
at Château d'Esclans is
only just beginning.
Sacha Lichine makes Château
d'Esclans the place to be, for every
festivity. A rosy kind of celebration
with a picture-perfect backdrop.

ROCK
Angel

The ideal dinner companions, Garrus and Whispering Angel by Sacha Lichine. In the center, Sacha with Susan Magrino and Mathilde Lichine.

Of course, evolving rosé from a silly, spring-break sensibility to sophisticated in the collective imagination was part and parcel of the Whispering Angel aesthetic, wholly embraced as a lifestyle of its own. Journalist Anna Galbraith perfectly sums up rosé's resonance: "It is unabashed, celebratory, and seemingly able to colour-match any given sunset. Perhaps just as importantly, it's now an unspoiled symbol of fun and frivolity— and, truly, we've never needed such a symbol more."

Beginning with Whispering Angel, a glass of rosé became synonymous with unpretentious summer ease à la française (or, from another perspective, an aspirational laid-back Hamptons life). But more broadly, rosé's abiding desirability has a direct line to the Provençal way of life. The unhurried pace, set to a pastel backdrop of fragrant lavender fields, lush vineyards, and painterly light, was popularized by beloved artists and writers, including the late English author Peter Mayle in his best-selling memoir *A Year in Provence*. Over the course of several generations, those depictions laid the groundwork for the region's eternal lure.

Rosé, by extension, is the embodiment of the lifestyle. In the fantasy, locals linger over salade Niçoise and herbally infused cuisine, loaf poolside with a bottle on ice, and play pétanque with friends until nightfall as the chorus of cicadas dims to a whisper. Moreover, no one in this fantasy takes themselves too seriously. The transportive and euphoric qualities inherent to rosé are threaded deeply into its widespread popularity. From the very first sip, rosé has the power—as all the best wines should—to lift the drinker out of their everyday circumstances and whisk them off to the sun-drenched beaches of Saint-Tropez or to the back of a boat cruising along the Mediterranean—even if only in their imaginations.

It is joie de vivre incarnate, which is why it so naturally extends to every occasion. Over the last fifteen years, it has become a fixture of celebratory affairs—from bridal showers and weddings to an elegant quaff for horse races and all-day picnics to intimate meals where its versatility with food shines bright.

Best of all, rosé isn't hemmed in by the snobbery or codified traditions of red and white wine consumption and can be enjoyed sans inhibition. Unlike nearly every other iconic beverage, there are few, if any, barriers to entry. Comedic essayist Sarah Miller wrote about how the world jumped so quickly on the rosé ship and that "its enjoyment was intertwined with the delicious smugness that comes with having good taste and knowing it."

If rosé became ubiquitous, transcending its role as a festive apéritif to take on millennial memes and merch, one cannot overlook the role that social media and celebrity culture have played. Social media sparked several years of rosé-inspired T-shirts and stickers, inflatable pool floats, and even flavored gummies, while a host of Hollywood stars followed in Sacha's footsteps to buy vineyards in the region and launch rosé brands of their own. As the fastest-growing beverage category with a high novelty quotient and massive reach, rosé had taken on a gimmicky side that led some to wonder whether the worldwide fanfare would be fleeting.

In the end was the silly #RoseAllDay trend, which peaked and faded almost as quickly as it emerged. What endures is an essential truth: rosé is a genuinely pleasurable drink that spices up everyday life. "It's the beach clubs and fun in the sun and beachy excess that are an undeniably sexy part of the whole culture that interests people," says Sacha of the vibe consumers can channel, no matter where they are. "But it lives on because there is truly good rosé to experience."

Sea, sun and endless summer in Miami, at The Setai and during Art Basel.
Following pages: Whispering Angel all summer long, the life of every party.

Pretty in pink:
These eminently drinkable, sophisticated dry wines with the most desirable sultry pale-pink tint informed if not a revolution, then a veritable lifestyle. It is joie de vivre incarnate, with its inherent transportive and euphoric qualities threading deeply into its widespread popularity.

A toast to the Provençal life, on the sun-drenched terraces and beaches of Loulou restaurant in Ramatuelle and of The Surf House in Montauk. A glass of rosé is synonymous with an unpretentious summer ease à la française.

Off to the races!
The Château d'Esclans rosés
have become a fixture of the
prestigious Goodwood horse
racing events as well as
St. Andrews Charity
Polo Tournament.

Whispering Angel

Painting the world pink, whether by land or by sea. From a day trip in the Saint-Tropez bay to the Monaco Yacht Show, Whispering Angel and Rock Angel are the perfect partners.

n the long history of wine, that rosé is a serious wine contender is still a relatively recent phenomenon, which means its long-lasting novelty and high pleasurability provide ample opportunities to develop the market further. Part of the Château d'Esclans vision is to take rosé beyond the confines of the summer and ski seasons and to make it a truly year-round staple.

"I always remember Bagatelle in Manhattan's meatpacking district would have diners drinking magnums of Whispering Angel on a Sunday in the middle of January. People would go for lunch, drink, party all afternoon, and by eight p.m. they'd be in bed ready to tackle the work week," recalls Sacha. "It may have been snowing outside, but for a day those people felt like they were in Saint-Tropez."

If he thinks back to the establishments, partnerships, and people that have helped put rosé and Château d'Esclans on the map, Sacha Lichine could easily close the chapter here. To an outsider, it might appear as if he has achieved it all, that he painted the world pink with the broadest strokes possible. Millions of bottles of his wines are produced each year and distributed in 106 countries. "I'm happy to see that we have demonstrated the more noble side to rosé, but if I'm being honest, the category is just beginning. There is so much left to be done and so much more to learn, so many different markets where we can still bring the revolution," insists the winemaker-entrepreneur-educator.

In other words, the history of Château d'Esclans is still being written.

CHÂTEAU D'ESCLANS

Whispering Angel at all the world's most important events for car enthusiasts: the Goodwood Festival of Speed in Chichester; the Grand Prix de Monaco; and The Bridge in Bridgehampton, New York.

Picturesque afternoons on the Mediterranean blend into spectacular summer evenings under the stars, sparkling with twinkle lights and Château d'Esclans rosés poured into every glass. Here, a special gathering for Sacha Lichine at Villa San Michele on Capri.

Picnic perfection, rosé style. Whispering Angel's versatility with food shines bright, whether at Galley Beach on Nantucket, Cape Cod, or in the Hamptons. The enduring truth about rosé is that it's a genuinely pleasurable drink that spices up everyday life.

The perfect match.
Whispering Angel is a
longtime official partner of the
Giorgio Armani Tennis Classic in
Hurlingham, UK, which celebrates
timeless elegance and quintessential
British traditions. The audience sips
rosé while watching the best tennis
players in the world prepare for
the prestigious Wimbledon
Tournament.

OFFICIAL PARTNER

Whispering Angel

As the pros take their swings, bottles of Whispering Angel are served at golf tournaments, like the so-very-British BMW PGA Championship at Wentworth Club.

Ski bunnies sip Whispering Angel on the slopes. From Switzerland's Alpina Gstaad, Olden Hotel and The Gstaad Palace, to Bulgaria's Kempinski Hotel Grand Arena in Bansko and New Zealand's mountains, rosé is the gold standard of après-ski.